MW00987040

ISBN-13: 978-0-9944557-0-3
ISBN-10: 0994455704

The Secret Art of Coffee Reading

Ancient Secrets Revealed

GULDJIN MILLER

DEDICATION

In loving memory of my beautiful mother, an angel on earth and now an angel in heaven. You captivated us all with your resonating light and left the world a much colder place. I miss you, I love you and I look forward to being with you again one day.

CONTENTS

GULDJIN MILLER

ACKNOWLEDGMENTS

Thank you to my Turkish family for passing on the many gifts I have been fortunate enough to receive. It has been a long but rewarding journey that I am very grateful to have travelled.

1. HISTORY OF COFFEE

One of the oldest coffee discovery legends tells of a young goat herder named Kaldi in Ethiopia in around 600 A.D. When he went looking for his herd, he noticed that after eating a certain kind of berry, they were particularly lively. He tasted the berries, and found that they increased his energy and also his alertness. Another man, named Acuba, noticed Kaldi and his herd's reaction to the berries, and decided to try it for himself. He realized the potential of this plant, and took them back to town where he mixed the berries with drinks at his monastery.

When the monks first tried the berry, which was actually a coffee bean, they were disappointed by its bitter flavor, and consequently threw it into the fire. Soon, a delicious aroma was wafting around and the monks used the coffee bean to create a brew which they saw as a gift from God, as it allowed them to stay awake half the night. Coffee then spread to other towns and monasteries, and Acuba became a rich man. No one knows what happened to Kaldi.

The coffee bean was kept a secret for several hundred years by the Arabs. Coffee eventually made its way into Western Europe and the Americas in the late 18th century.

Initially, Arabs brewed coffee from green, un-roasted beans, making a tea-like beverage. By the late 13th century, Arabians roasted and ground coffee before brewing it. The use of coffee beans spread throughout the Arabian Peninsula, and later via the Ottoman Empire to Turkey. When the Turks broke their siege in Vienna in 1683, they left behind 500 sacks of coffee. A Polish businessman saw this product's potential and opened up the world's first coffee house, and this then opened up the "world of coffee" to the masses. That is when "cup-women" (as they were known) appeared. If you required wisdom, you would consult one of these women, and they would provide you with the answers to your future.

Consequently, coffee cup readings became very popular – and notorious – with official notifications to ban the activity. Initially, these types of readers stated their trade in Paris, and then worked their way across to Germany.

Coffee readings are psychic readings done by using a cup of coffee as though it's a crystal ball. Ground Turkish coffee is mostly used when cup readings are done. The residue is left at the bottom of the cup after the coffee is drunk. Then the cup is covered with a saucer, and then turned over (upside down) onto the saucer. The cup is then lifted, and placed onto a paper towel/tissue to dry.

The patterns formed on the inside of the cup reveal a "story" and insight into the person's life. It also triggers psychic insight, and the patterns are interpreted according to what they mean to the seer. When viewing the patterns, one must open up their intuition to receive "messages" and with a little training and practice, the skill of reading coffee cups will be developed.

If a coffee cup is drunk in a hurry or by someone who is not relaxed, the cup will not be able to be read. The sediment will not form any meaningful patterns – merely chaotic brown dots and mud in a cup! This is probably true of any type of readings, and if the focus or intention is not present, the medium used will not provide a useful insight into the future.

2. READING YOUR MORNING COFFEE

Traditionally, either Turkish or Greek coffee has been used when performing coffee readings. The coffee is grounded up into a fine powder as this produces the best results for reading as it creates clear patterns and symbols within the cup. However, it is possible to read other types of coffee.

Ideally, it is preferable to have coffee with milk as this tends to leave more patterns within your cup. Latte's and cappuccino's are great due to the foam of the milk but most coffees will give you some symbols you can read. Alternatively, for those of you wanting a break from coffee, most hot chocolates will leave patterns in your cup due to the milk content and can be read just as effectively.

Something else to keep in mind is that patterns are not only left on the inside of the cup. Coffee marks on the outside of the cup can also be read as these symbols are just as important (we'll get into this with more detail a little later on). They too can tell a 'story' and are very beneficial in informing you about what is coming up for you very soon – if not right now.

As you proceed through this book, you will note that much of what I discuss is directed towards Turkish coffee however these can easily be used for reading 'regular' coffee. The same principles apply.

Many people take their coffee 'to go' and so drink it directly out of a take away cup. A fundamental rule is that readings should always commence at the handle. This gives you the timeline (again, explained more in detail further on in this book). Take away cups usually do not have handles but usually have lids, to avoid spillage. I recommend the starting point to be the point opposite the opening of the lid (where you drink from).

If you have a take away cup without a lid, I would recommend the starting point to be the join in the paper cup. This is the best place to start when you do not have a handle.

Something important to remember when you first start reading coffee cups is that it does take practice.

The more cups you read, the better you will get. I have provided detailed methods on how to open your 'third' eye and increase your psychic ability. EVERYONE has psychic ability; it's just that some of us know how to tap into it easily whilst others require some guidance. This book will help you with opening your channels.

I have included a detailed glossary at the back of the book which will provide you with meanings. Please remember - you must always trust your own instincts, first and foremost, when reading coffee cups as your intuition will never steer you wrong. This is very important.

I have provided some examples of symbols (below) that may appear in your cup, to assist you when you commence reading:

In the picture (next page), it shows a woman facing away (from the left). Above her head, there is a small dot, which appears to be a bird (if you look very closely). This represents that news will be received when she least expects it. As it is all clear around her, it will be good news.

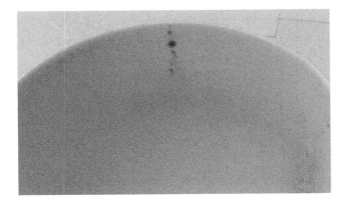

Again, it may not be clear straight away to you but please be patient. Also, you must trust your instincts when looking at pictures. It is important to see what is around the picture as this can also give you more detail as to what is going on. When there aren't many things around it and it looks 'clear', this means that things will be positive. If there were many lines or dark patterns around, this represents problems and a darkness (meaning negative issues).

When reading a coffee cup, it is very important to trust your own instincts. Also, as you develop your psychic abilities, you will see more and be able to provide more detail.

In the picture on the next page, you can see a large bouquet of flowers (middle):

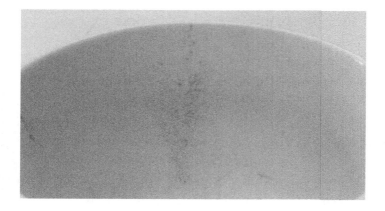

This represents that the coffee drinker will be receiving a bouquet of flowers soon. I know that it will be soon as this picture was near the handle.

As the picture is light in color and there is no other symbols close by, this represents that the flowers will be happily received.

Also, as you become more experienced, you will be able to tell who will be sending the flowers, why and what the outcome of this will be. Again, as you gain more experience and learn to open your third eye, you will be amazed at what you will be able to see.

As you proceed through this book, it will provide you with more detail as to how cups are to be read, in regards to placement of symbols, timelines and meanings. This book is predominately based on Turkish coffee but the guidelines can be used to read any type of coffee.

You can read your cup each day to let you know what to expect, and again, the more you practice, the better (and easier) this whole process will become.

Ok, so let's begin the process of reading Turkish coffee. This is the traditional method of reading coffee cups and the rest of this book will focus on this technique but again, everything relating to Turkish coffee can be used to read all other types of coffee.

Enjoy and have fun!!

3. GETTING STARTED

The items you need to begin reading Turkish coffee are some Turkish or Greek coffee, a jezve or ibrik (milk jug), a coffee cup and saucer, and sugar (optional). All of these items can be purchased from your local supermarket or a Continental food store.

There are various types of Turkish coffee.   I have found that the best coffee to read is the light colored variety. Usually Greek coffee is lighter, so if this is available, I would recommend purchasing this. I find that the contrasts between "light and dark pictures" in the cup are clearer to distinguish between.   If only the dark variety is available, don't worry, this is fine.

A jezve or ibrik is a small saucer used to cook the coffee. If you visit a Continental shop, tell them that you want to use it to make coffee, and they should be able to help you out. Alternatively, you can use a milk saucepan from your local supermarket.

Turkish coffee cups and saucers are quite small compared to your traditional mugs used for standard coffee. Espresso cups are basically the same size (maybe a little bit bigger). I have found that old English tea cups are perfect, as they are still relatively small but as they are similar to an upside down "V," this makes reading coffee cups much easier. If you cannot find these from your local supermarket, a good continental food store will definitely have them.

Making the Coffee

1. Fill the coffee cup with cold water;
2. Pour the cold water into the jezve;
3. Add one heaped tablespoon of Turkish coffee and one teaspoon of sugar* (for one cup of coffee) – sugar is optional;
4. Stir until mixed together, and heat on cook top;
5. The coffee mixture should be placed on a medium heat, otherwise the coffee will not cook properly;
6. Stir occasionally;
7. The coffee will develop froth on the top which is called "gaymuk" (pronounced guymuck). This gives the coffee a nicer taste;
8. Let the coffee rise and remove from stove;
9. Stir and place back on stove to rise again;
10. Pour a little into each cup to ensure that each cup receives some froth;

11. Pour the remaining coffee into the cup/s.

(*Note: If sugar is required, it must be added now as the sugar must be "cooked" with the coffee, otherwise sugar granules will appear in the cup if added at the end).

Drinking the Coffee

I have been asked by many people regarding the correct way to drink Turkish coffee. Should they use a particular hand? Do they need to drink from a certain side of the cup? Some people believe that you should use your left hand, as this is linked to your heart. I personally feel that it does not matter how you hold the cup, or whether you drink with either hand. Your fortune will come out the same way regardless, but if you feel more comfortable with drinking your coffee using a certain hand – go ahead. You should do what you feel is "right" for you.

Traditionally, the coffee is served with a glass of rosewater. As many people do not like the taste of rosewater, I serve water with my Turkish coffee. As the coffee has a "thick" texture, many people like to have a glass of water on hand to help remove some of the "grittiness." If you are a lover of coffee, you will enjoy the taste of Turkish coffee, and will not need a glass of water.

When is the cup ready to turn over?

The cup is ready to be turned over when you find a thick layer of coffee at the bottom. Be careful not to leave too much of the "drinkable" coffee in the cup (this is the thin liquid in the cup). If you do, you will find that, when turning over your cup, you will remove the thick layer of coffee out of the cup and into the saucer.

Once you are comfortable that you are unable to drink any more of your coffee, as there is a thick, gritty layer of sediment on the bottom of the cup, you can now turn your cup over. Be careful – ensure that the cup is sitting flat on the plate; otherwise the contents will fall out.

Turning over the cup

Place the saucer over the top of the cup;

Place your thumb on the bottom of the cup, and your index finger on the saucer:

Make a wish, and move the cup in a clockwise motion in front of you (three times);

Turn the cup over, and place it on the table.

Any hand can be used for this process.

WARNING – Be careful when turning the cup over, as I have seen many spillages in my time. When turning the cup over, make sure that it is kept close to your body, and that it is done in one quick motion. I have seen coffee spilled all down a wall once by an overzealous friend, and have had to clean many large coffee stains off carpet due to the saucer not sitting on the cup properly when the cup was turned over. It may be worth turning your cup over a table when first doing this if you are not very confident. Many of you will not have a problem, but I thought it best to warn you for those of you who do not have a steady hand.

Place a tissue next to the cup, remove the cup off the saucer, and place onto the tissue. This will assist the cup to dry. DO NOT TIP THE CUP OVER TO HAVE A LOOK. If the cup is turned over when transferring to the tissue, you will find that the wet coffee inside will move, and it will distort the sediment inside of the cup. This will affect your reading, so I highly recommend that you do not do this.

GULDJIN MILLER

4. RECOGNIZING SYMBOLS AND SHAPES

If when you look at the clouds, you are able to see shapes of animals, people, etc. – then you will be able to read coffee cups. The whole art to reading coffee is the interpretation of pictures.

When you first look in to the cup, you may think to yourself, "I cannot see a single thing except for a lot of squiggly lines." But as you continue to look at the coffee, you may suddenly notice a picture of a bird or a flower. The more you look, the more you should see and the more you practice, the better you will get.

I have found that when someone is very confused, their cup is usually just full of "squiggles," and no matter how hard you look, you will not be able to see many pictures. I find that if this person clears their mind and has another coffee, you will find that usually their cup will "clear," and you will be able to see many pictures and symbols. If it doesn't, it may be best to get them to have a coffee another day or when they sort out some of their problems.

As you become more experienced, you may find that when you pick up someone's cup, you may have a "flash" or strong feeling regarding something which may have already happened or something which is about to happen. It took me a few years to develop this skill, so don't be discouraged if this doesn't happen to you straight away. If you are in tune with your intuition, this may happen quite quickly. Everyone learns at a different rate, so don't compare yourself to anyone else.

Sometimes you may see a symbol which I have not mentioned in my index of symbols, and wonder what it represents. Look at the symbols around it, and use your own intuition. If you still can't work it out, leave it and maybe next time it pops up you may be able to work out what it represents.

Signs to look for before reading the cup

When you have turned your cup over, you may have noticed "bubbles" coming out of the cup and onto the saucer. This represents that people are gossiping about you.

If there are bubble/s on the top of your cup as you

are drinking, this means that someone is thinking of you in a positive way.

If, when you go to pick up your upturned cup from the saucer and the cup is "stuck," meaning that the cup will not detach from the saucer, this means that you are not meant to have your cup read at that moment. This is not necessarily a bad sign. It only means that something is going to occur that you are not meant to know in advance. It is best to leave your cup today and try again tomorrow.

If, when reading a cup and the cup "jumps" out of your hands, the last thing you said will not happen.

If the cup jumps from your hands and breaks – do not panic. It means that you are continually looking in cups for the same answer to a situation or problem, and have been given the answer time and time again. Do not read any other cups until you get over your "obsession." Alternatively, if this is not the case, something bad was going to happen to you, but will no longer happen as the "negative" energy was absorbed by the cup, and everything will be fine. You will know which applies to you.

A symbol on the handle of the cup represents something happening right at this moment involving your family.

A symbol on the rim of the cup (on the outside)

represents what is either happening right now or has just happened. If you see an "eye" on the rim of your cup, this represents that someone is watching you. If the eye is light in color, this presents someone with blue/green eyes (light colored eyes). If the eye is dark in color, this represents someone with dark colored eyes. This is fairly basic, so if you apply this theory to your cup reading, you will understand the fundamentals of cup reading.

Long line/s (light in color) on the outside represents shedding a tear of joy. If dark in color, it will be a tear of sadness.

If a symbol is on the bottom of the cup (outside), it represents that something is being hidden from you. The symbol may give you an indication of what it is.

5. LOOKING IN THE CUP

Turn the cup over and take a look inside. Start at the handle. As a guide, I will reference a clock. The handle should be at 12 o'clock. This position represents right now. Whatever you see at this point, is happening now or about to happen. The cup itself works on a 12 month clock. At "3 o'clock," this represents 3 months; 6 o'clock represents 6 months, and so on. Symbols at the bottom of the cup represent the cup drinker's family.

Sometimes there is a dark 'blob' down the bottom which represents that someone in your family is keeping something hidden. Also, a raised bump of coffee represents that you will receive a surprise that will make you jump. To tell whether the surprise will be positive or negative, have a look at the symbols close by as they will be able to let you know what you can expect.

(Below) we start at the handle and take a look slightly to the left. There are two people meeting and as it is almost on the handle (coming from the left), this represents a meeting with someone from your past. As the handle represents the "beginning." As the cup is clear after the meeting (white space), this represents that it will be a good meeting.

As we progress our way through the cup (next page), the symbol is located at the 3 month mark (a quarter of the way around the cup) – 3 o'clock – there is a half shaped star. A star represents a wish coming true, but as the star is only half visible, this represents that a wish will partially come true. You will not receive exactly what you want, but you will receive part of it. There also appears to be an eye in the middle of the star. This represents that someone is watching this wish closely. It can also represent that they are a bit jealous of this wish coming true.

(Next page), at around the 5-6 month point, you will see a picture of a person holding a document (if using a 12 hour clock, this person is located at 11 o'clock). As the document is light in color, this represents that it will be positive. The person appears to be skipping (jumping), so they look happy.

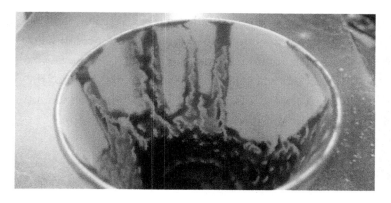

As we continue to work around the cup (below), you will see a light outline of a person facing away from the handle (directly to the left). This represents that someone from your past is thinking of you (ghost from the past). This is someone who has been out of your life for a while. As it is quite light around them, this would be a positive experience for the person who is having their cup read.

As we arrive back at the handle, we take a look at the bottom of the cup. This represents the person who is having their cup read and their family. In the cup below, you will see an angelfish at the bottom of the cup. A fish represents money. An angelfish would represent an inheritance, as an angel represents someone who has passed away.

So......that was a very basic reading. As you become more experienced with reading coffee, you will notice more shapes within the cup. In the beginning, you will see simple shapes, and you can interpret the meaning of the symbols by using the guide at the back of this book. With practice, you will start to provide more detail on the symbols (pictures) that you see.

6. READINGS

I have included some sample readings to help you with your coffee reading journey. My clients were kind enough to give their permission to include their personal readings to provide you with some additional guidance on what to look for and how to create a "flow" when reading a cup.

The following cup was for a young man who wanted a "general reading." He was new to coffee reading, and was unsure of what to expect. He had some reservations, but that is not necessarily a bad thing. Doubt can sometimes enhance a reading, and it's ok if you are faced with the same issue. More often than not, people walk away from a reading being completely amazed at how information can be retrieved from "squiggly" dark coffee grounds.

Reading 1:

For this reading, there were no symbols on the outside of the cup, so that is why we start at the handle (below). There is "open" space with little dots (at 1 o'clock). These dots represent news coming to this young man. As it is light and the area is clear, the news is good.

On the next page (at 2 o'clock from handle), you can see the young man climbing up – he is lying quite low (which means that he is working hard to move up in the world). He reaches the top, and is looking to see what is available to him and where he can go from here. The area around him is clear, so his prospects look positive. He is also leaning forward, so he is waiting for some news.

At 3 o'clock from the handle it shows the young man in an embrace with someone else. We are at the 3 month mark, so he will be sharing a romantic kiss with someone around this time. Their bodies seem entwined, so it will be an intense moment. As the girl's legs seem to be around him, this indicates that the girl will be more attracted to him (and more intense) than he is.

In the picture below, we are still at the 3 month mark, but you can see two birds talking to each other (just to the left of 3 o'clock). This represents two people sharing news. He will find out good news (for himself), and he will then pass on some good news to someone else.   It is good news due to it being "light" in color in the cup.

The cup is quite light at this point, and so this represents that the young man will have good things coming to him at this stage. As we move around to the 6 month mark (next picture), you will see a line up the top of the cup. This line represents communication from a distance. Phone call, text, email, or skype. As the line is long, it represents that the communication is from another city, not a local call.

At 7 o'clock from the handle in the next picture shows the young man finding out that someone has kept something hidden. The person is wearing a hat and opening a large box. Under this box is a couple kissing, so the secret seems to be about this couple. Next to the box, you can see a light outline of the boy (in white). This looks to be the girl the young man was previously kissing. She is actually with someone else or caught kissing someone else and this has been kept a secret from the young man (by the person wearing the hat). However, this is now coming out into the open and upset the young man as the coffee becomes darker in color.

As we continue to look at this picture, I can see that someone will find out about this betrayal (and the fact that someone else knows about this betrayal), and they will be surprised that nothing has been said (see picture below at 9 o'clock from handle). They are leaning in to see what is going on (over the shoulder of the person), and can see that the other person is hiding this fact. I can see that finding out this information creates heaviness on their mind, and they are unsure of what to say (or to say anything at all to this young man – which looks to be his friend).

This will be a controversial event (around the 9 month mark), and things seem to get busier in the cup. Behind the person who is looking over the shoulder of the man with the hat, I can see a person holding a chicken. A chicken represents something productive, the beginning of something new. The girl behind is holding a chicken tightly, meaning if she lets go, this will create a new beginning.

As we have progressed back to the 12 month mark,

the cup was clear and so we move down to the bottom of the cup. The bottom of the cup represents events within the family (except is there is a bump which means that the coffee drinker will be receiving a shock shortly).

The bottom of the cup has a large lump which looks like an eclipse. This means that there has been something happening in this person's life that has been negative and "dragging him down," but it is passing now, and underneath it looks clear, so things will improve for the better.

After reading the bottom of the cup, the coffee drinker makes a (silent) wish, and presses their thumb down the bottom. The mark is then read to interpret whether the wish will come true, and what events will be happening in regards to the wish. (Below) I can see two people, hidden in the darkness, exchanging something, which is the white round circle (representing something positive). This looks positive.

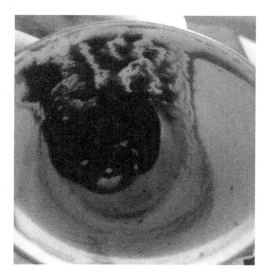

I can not see a clear circle, so it is uncertain if the wish will come true, but the wish is quite hidden (due to the darkness). There aren't any breaks in the wish, so that is a good sign for the wish.

*Please note - if you are unable to see any of these pictures, that is ok. We all interpret things differently, and with practise you will be amazed at what you can see.

Reading 2:

The cup below was for a single middle aged woman. She has some patterns on the outside of her cup, and so we start the cup reading with these.

The symbols outside of the cup represent events that are about to happen (or have just happened).

Here we can see two lines, and one is longer and lighter than the other. She will be going on two significant paths/roads (not necessarily holidays). These could signify an event in their life. The first line represents that she will take an enjoyable "road," and she will find out key things (the dots on the path). The last dot looks like a love heart, so she will be hearing about love.

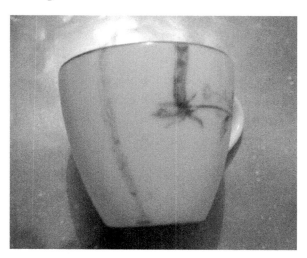

The second path is shorter and more prominent.

There looks to be a person standing there with their
hands in front of them waiting for something. It
looks like there is a bird above their head, meaning
they will be receiving some news they have been
waiting for.

We always commence at the handle and work our way
around the cup clockwise. Just to the left of the
handle (which means this may have just happened), I
see two people bending down and above them is a big
rooster. A rooster means that there will be (or was) a
significant argument between the two. As they are
kneeling down, this means that the argument really hit
hard (the words said were quite harsh). Beneath this,
there are quite a few dark "squiggles',"which means
that the person having the cup read was/is worried
about what happened. Then we continue to move
towards the right, and can see that things start to clear

up. The next cup shows a busy time for the woman. She seems to be walking away from a situation (at 2 o'clock from handle), as she is walking back towards the handle. If she was walking towards a situation, she would be moving through the cup as we read it (clockwise).

The situation that she appears to be walking away from has quite a bit happening. There seems to be a bit of confusion (hence the many "squiggles"), and there is a dollar sign with a bird sitting on it (at 3 o'clock from handle). This represents confusion in regards to money. She will get some news about a large sum of money, but she does not want to know about it (hence walking away) – I later found out that she had recently seperated from her husband and was going through a messy divorce, particularly with their finances.

Next to this is a high pile of papers (5 o'clock from handle), so our coffee drinker will have a mountain of paperwork to deal with.

As we continue to move through the cup, this "messy" period passes and things start to clear up. However, halfway down the cup, there seems to be quite a bit of "squiggly" lines, which means that she is worried about events. As the coffee is quite light, her worries are more due to herself stressing, and less due to the seriousness of her situation.

She will have three significant conversations (meetings) with people. A meeting does not necessarily mean a work meeting, but rather a meeting of two people. This could mean a lunch meeting or social meeting, etc. They are light in color, and so will be a positive experience for her (at 9 o'clock).

Now that we have made it back to the handle, we look down at the bottom of the cup. As there wasn't anything of significance on the bottom, we progress to the wish. The woman made her wish (in her head, as we are not allowed to know it), and pressed her thumb on the bottom of the cup. *Note- if the person's thumb nail is too long or they are unable to use their thumb, they can use another finger (although the thumb is preferable).

Looking at the picture (on the next page), you will see that the circle is quite prominent, however, not fully complete. As the circle is not complete, this represents that the woman's wish will not come true. There seems to be an issue with it coming true. Most of it is complete, and then it seems to not happen.

The circle in the middle is quite clear, so there is a possibility of this coming true if she changes her tactics.

Reading 3:

The next reading was for a young lady who was quite anxious about getting married to her long term boyfriend.

We commence the cup on the outside. There are two lines (see the cup on the next page), and the line on the right hand side appears to have a cacoon which represents that she is about to "blossom." She can expect some great changes in her life very soon (if it is not happening already). As the cacoon is light in color, the changes will be positive.

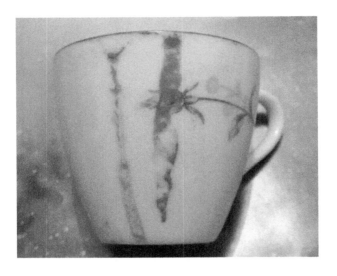

As we enter the cup, it seems very full with many pictures, which means that there is a lot happening in this woman's life.

Immediately after the handle (next page), you can see the woman reaching for a pot, and it seems just out of her hands. She is really stretching to reach this, and the contents look like something positive and something she really wants. She is standing on an upside down love heart (which means she is confused about love). I would interpret this to represent her getting engaged. If she just "hangs in there," she will receive what she is wanting very soon. As it is close to the handle, this event is closer than she realises.

As we move through the cup, towards the three month mark, we see a light bird wearing a hat (next page –between 2 & 3 o'clock). This represents news in disguise. She will hear some positive news she wasn't meant to hear. As the bird is quite plump, it will be quite a bit of news.

(Below - at 5 o'clock near the top) there is a person holding a large sword. This represents an enemy who will fall (fail).

It looks like they were trying to do something behind her back (see the picture of them behind her back at 9 o'clock – lower in the cup - below). They will not win.

(Below), there is an anchor which seems to be pulled out and leaning to the right. This means that it is not secure, and so this person will be moving their house. If the anchor was facing down, it would mean she was staying put. There seems to be something attached to the anchor, which on closer inspection, means that with the move, she will be taking some "baggage" with her. As she is getting divorced and leaving the family home, this will mean that the move will result in some baggage for her and will not be "clear cut."

Towards the left of the handle at 10 o'clock (below) shows a large hat. This means that something large has been hidden, and will be revealed to her in about 10 months.

(Above – at 12 o'clock – near the bottom of the cup - it shows a dark arrow pointing up. An arrow represents direction. This one is quite large, and will provide her with much needed guidance. It will be a significant change for her.

We have worked around the cup, and have now arrived at the bottom of the cup. There was nothing to read, there was only dark sediment. The woman was asked to make a wish and press her thumb at the bottom. Viewing the wish, it is quite white, which meansthat it is clear for her and there will not be any

major issues. To the left of the wish, there is a ring
with a bow on it. That represents a promise which
will feel like a gift to the woman. She will be very
happy. There is no clear ring print, so it's difficult to
give a certain yes or no as to whether her wish will
come true, but there will not be many issues to
contend with.

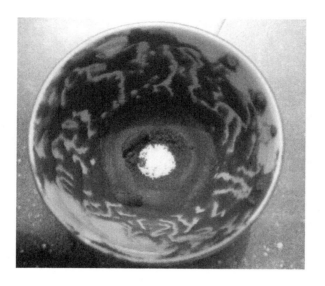

Please note – any finger can be used when pressing
down at the bottom of the cup. If you have
particularly long nails, you can press your thumb into
the coffee left on the coffee plate and press this onto
the outside of the cup for your wish to be read.

GULDJIN MILLER

7. WORKING WITH YOUR THIRD EYE

Many people believe that only a select group of fortunate people are born with the gift to know what the future holds. This is not completely true. What separates these unique people from the masses is that they have learned how to open up their "third eye" so they can receive messages from the other side.

In this chapter, I will provide some guidance on how to open and develop your third eye so as to assist you in reading cups successfully.

The first and most effective technique that I would recommend is Meditation.

Meditation encourages us to switch off our analytical, everyday-thinking-brain and tap into our intuitive, creative, subconscious mind. This allows us to access information on a deep level, and is essential in psychic development. When we start to analyze our feelings and the things that pop into our heads, we block the messages that are being sent via our intuition or from spirit. It is important that we are able to switch into this mode easily, as this will allow us to access our psychic abilities.

Meditation isn't difficult or complicated; it can be as simple as relaxing in an armchair and listening to your favorite piece of calm music. There are some people whose minds are quite "scattered" and full with chatter. This technique will really help calm your nervous energy and center your focus. A form of meditation is yoga. I have found yoga to be really beneficial in calming my busy mind, and it has helped me to stay "centered."

One meditation technique that you can practice is to relax in a comfortable chair or bed. Switch off the TV, radio, and all phones (both mobile and landline). Darken the room, wear loose clothing, and close your eyes.

To release the day's stresses, inhale deeply and slowly. Breathe in through your nose, and exhale through your mouth. Repeat these processes until you feel the tension drain from your body and you feel calm and relaxed.

Now, hold an attitude of total rejection in your mind. You need to reject the whole world, and all the negative thoughts that can weaken you.

Next, you need to clear your mind completely by stating that there is nothing that you want, and therefore you will think of nothing and your mind will go completely blank. This is a basic form of hypnosis or auto-suggestion to enable you to affect the desired mental conditions, with very little effort on your part.

To deepen the hypnotic state, concentrate on the third eye, located in the square-inch space between the eyes, as this will alter your brain waves to alpha, allowing Magnetic Psychic Power to manifest.

An indication that you are succeeding will be a sudden and unexpected release of disconnected visual images. These are the excreta of the relaxed brain.

The next step is to sit quietly for a few minutes, then count to five slowly, and with each count lift yourself higher, becoming lighter and lighter letting yourself awaken refreshed, bright, full of energy and optimism, feeling happier. On the count of five, become wide awake. You might like to pretend that you are at the bottom of the sea, and need to force yourself up to the surface.

In order to successfully gain access to your third eye, it is essential to resolve any stress or issues within your life. We all have daily stresses such as bills and general living, so unfortunately, for most of us, that is unavoidable. However, more issues such as differences between you and those around you can hinder your psychic ability. It is difficult to tune into your psychic abilities unless you feel peace within yourself and with others. Avoid fighting in general, and be quick to resolve conflict within your life. Learn to argue constructively, working towards a final resolution. Merely trying to hurt each other in anger only makes a problem worse. Meditating is more difficult when you have the burden of personal drama on your shoulders.

A technique called Clairsentience is also beneficial for opening your third eye. This technique focusses on receiving intuitive information via feelings. A great way to increase this ability is through touch by reading the energy of objects. A simple way to do this is:

1. Ask someone to bring you small objects that you can practice on.

2. It's beneficial if the item is small enough to fit inside your hands. Jewelry and keys are great, as metal holds energy well. A piece of jewelry which is regularly worn, such as a wedding ring or bracelet, has a lot more energy than an item that is rarely worn. However, do not restrict yourself to jewelry. A piece of clothing or any other personal item that can

be worn is just as useful. However, when you are starting out, I would recommend sticking to metal jewelry.

3. Now, situate yourself in a comfortable position, somewhere quiet. Take a few deep breaths, and rub your hands together to get the energy moving within your body.

4. Take the object, and place this in your hands. Close your eyes and continue to take deep breaths (breathe in through your nose and breathe out through your mouth). Now start to pay attention to how your body is feeling. Do you feel anything? Do you see or hear anything? Do not disregard anything that comes to you. If you don't feel, see, or hear anything, it's ok. You may be feeling stuck or even "blank." Ways to try and "move" things is by asking yourself some questions:

    a. Does the object belong to a man or a woman?
    b. Is the owner of this object happy or sad?
    c. What personality traits does the person have?
    d. What do they do for a living?

5. If you are performing this in front of someone, ask them for some feedback, as this will help lead you in the right direction. If you are on your own, write down ANYTHING that comes to mind. Do not filter any of the information while you are performing this task. The point of this exercise is to get you used to receiving energetic impressions.

6. Ask the person who gave you the object for feedback to see if you were able to pick up any correct information. This includes anything you heard, saw or felt. It's important to have confidence when performing this, otherwise you will close off your "senses," and then this will just make the whole process much harder.

Using playing cards to develop your skills:

Another simple technique, which I used quite a bit when I first started developing my psychic abilities, was the use of playing cards.

1. Take a pack of playing cards.
2. Turn them face down, and pick up a card without looking at it.
3. Clear your mind.

4. Now focus on the card, and the first number that pops into your head is the one you state.
5. The more you practice, the better you will get.

Overcoming your fears of the psychic world is crucial to opening your psychic abilities. Psychic contact and other supernatural phenomena can be frightening, but fear hinders abilities even more than negativity. If you want to get in touch with your spiritual side, you can't be afraid of the consequences. If you fear contact with the spirit world, you will not "hear" or "see" the messages that they will want to give you. You may see new things when you least expect it, and so you must remain open and happy when these things are given to you. Being grateful when messages are given will ensure that more messages and insight will be given to you in the future. Being grateful is VERY important, so please ensure that when you receive messages that you thank the spirit world for providing these to you. A simple "thank you" once you have completed a reading or when you have received a random message is just plain good manners.

One tip that I feel is the most important is – do not misuse your psychic ability for personal gain. I'm sure that there are some of you who are thinking "well, what's the use of having it if you can't benefit from it?" Well, the answer is that you are given this gift in order to help other people. If you provide readings and people pay you, that is ok, as you have provided them with some guidance and, more often than not, helped reduce their stress and worry. It is when you use your psychic gifts in a selfish manner, for example, if you bet money after psychically predicting who will win a horse race or to win on the roulette table, prepare to lose.

Finally, my last tip is - do not get discouraged if you do not perform very well in the beginning. It's all about practice. The more you practice, the better you will become.

8. PSYCHIC MIND POWERS

There are three techniques that you can master to stimulate the psychic powers of your mind. These, if used correctly, can help you to discover the secret thoughts and actions of others, protect you from evil, and allow you to perfect your cup readings.

Practice each technique for five minutes every day, whenever convenient for you, until you have the psychic power under total control and can generate it automatically. These rites may seem simple, but they are carefully designed to help you tune in, and turn on, the psychic part of your mind.

PSYCHIC VISION:

This is the power of the Psychic Mind that is sometimes called "distant viewing" or "awareness projection." It deals with the ability to see through walls and over great distances, to gain secret knowledge.

To turn on your Psychic Vision:

1. Lie down in a dark, quiet room. Close your eyes and concentrate on an object, e.g. vase, statue, picture. The target object should be at least two feet away. Try to see the object clearly, as if you had your eyes open.

2. Now shift your awareness one step beyond the object, and examine the spot. Study every minute detail, and make a mental note of what you see.

3. Open your eyes. Then get up and go to the spot that you visited to see how well you did.

Practice this technique for five minutes every day until you can shift your awareness anywhere within a range of ten feet and still maintain perfect psychic visions of objects and people.

Develop the ability to see through walls and doors:

1. Turn on your Psychic Vision.

2. Picture in your mind a relative or friend, and stand beside them. Take notice of the surroundings. Accept whatever you see. Then bring your awareness back, and open your eyes.

3. Go to the location and check for accuracy.
    Do not let any initial inaccuracies deter you
    from continuing to develop this power of the
    mind. Practice will improve the accuracy of
    your observations. These simple experiments
    have generated the psychic power to leave
    your body, at will.

PYSCHIC HEARING:

Most commonly known as "telepathy," a psychic
hearing allows you to probe the most intimate secrets
of others, discover who your true friends really are,
punish your enemies, attract new friends and lovers,
receive telepathic messages from thousands of miles
away, and build a better life for yourself, by tuning in
to golden opportunities and investment tips.

To turn on your Psychic Hearing:

1. Lie down in a dark, quiet room. Close your
    eyes, and let your mind go completely blank.
    Think of an inky darkness filling your mind
    like a foggy mist.

2. Next try to imagine a golden light starting to
    seep through the darkness, right at its center,
    and then imagine it as glowing brighter until it
    illuminates the entire inside of your head.
    The golden light is pure telepathic power.

3. Concentrate on the golden light for five minutes every day, until it shines bright and clear each time you create it.

Practice this technique for five minutes every day, until you can do it automatically and generate the Telepathic Mind Sphere in 30 seconds or less. Once you have mastered this technique of generating the golden sphere, you are ready to begin using it to discover the secret thoughts and actions of others.

Develop your Psychic Hearing:

1. Generate the Telepathic Mind Sphere.

2. Imagine that the golden sphere of light is slowly starting to expand outside your head, until it fills the room so that you will be able to "hear" the secret thoughts of anyone standing near you.

3. Practice filing the room with the golden light, over and over. After a while, you will notice it becomes automatic and can be generated instantly in 30 seconds or less.

    This process may seem simple, but it has just filled you with telepathic power. With practice daily, you will be amazed at how easily you will be able to read the mind of anyone you want to.

PSYCHIC FORCE:

This is a power of the mind also known as "Telekinesis," which is the rare ability to move solid objects by mind power alone.

To turn on your Psychic Force:

1. Lie down in a dark, quiet room. Close your eyes, and concentrate on blackness. Think of your mind filled with a dense, black mist.

2. Now imagine a tiny point a glowing red light, like a tiny star, right in the center of your head. This inner light is psychic force, and there is no limit to its power.

3. Concentrate on the red point for five minutes every day, until it shines bright and clear whenever your mind creates it and the space it occupies is filled with a bright red glow.

This ritual will turn your kinetic mind powers on. After two weeks of repeated practice, you will notice a feeling of mental well-being as you continue the training process, and your mind will be literally crackling as the kinetic energies of Psychic Force are stimulated.

Develop your Psychic Force:

1. Lie down in a darkened room, and make yourself as comfortable as possible. This is vital, as you're going to need all the mental energy you can bring into focus.

2. Turn on your Psychic Force and concentrate on the red light. Slowly, start to leak energy from your mind into the red glow. Keep adding more and more until it seems to be finally reaching a blinding, intense red light. This is only mental imagery, and there is no danger of it causing any harm to you.

3. Practice generating this mental inferno over and over, until you can do it in just a few seconds.

GULDJIN MILLER

9.   QUESTIONS & ANSWERS

1. **How much of my coffee do I need to drink before I turn my cup over?**
    It's important to leave some sediment at the bottom of the cup so you will be able to have a good reading. Drink most of your coffee, and once you reach the thick sediment, stop and turn your cup over onto your small plate.

2. **I tried to lift my cup up, once I had turned it over, and it was stuck to my plate. Is it ok to force it off?**
    If this happens, most readers will not read your cup, as this often means that the cup does not want to be read as there is something you are not meant to know. This does not necessarily mean that the news is bad, more that some things are better left unknown......for now.

3. **I noticed a couple of bubbles on the top of my coffee? What does that mean?**

   Bubbles on the top of your coffee means that people are talking about you. The more bubbles, the more things people are saying.

4. **I left my coffee and it became cold, before drinking it, and the sediment became very watery. Is it ok to turn over?**

   It is fine to turn over but you won't get very good shapes, so I would recommend drinking another cup.

5. **When I was reading a cup, it "jumped" out of my hands. What does that mean?**

   If the coffee cup does this, it means whatever the last thing was read, this will no longer happen.

6. **When I about to turn over my cup onto the plate, do I have to swirl the cup around or can I just turn it over and leave it?**

   Some people like to swirl the cup three times before turning it over, while other do not perform this. Either way is correct. It really does not make much difference. Some people swirl their cup three times while making a wish. This is optional.

7. **I was reading a cup, and it slipped out of my hands and broke. Does this mean something bad will happen?**
Don't worry – this just means that the cup does not want to be read at this time, which is not necessarily bad. Best to leave it for now and try again at another time.

8. **The cup is full of squiggly lines and I can't see any shapes?**
Often when the cup drinker is very stressed or worried about something, their cup can be full of squiggly lines. Their confusion causes this, and makes it near impossible to read. You can either get them to take a few deep breathes to calm their thoughts and drink another cup, or you can leave it for another day.

9. **I don't like coffee. Do I have to drink the coffee to have a reading?**
It's preferable to drink the coffee; however, you don't have to. I have drunk a coffee on behalf of someone (I think of them as I drink the cup), and then I read the cup for them. This can be very successful. However, it takes a bit of practice.

10. **Is it ok to read a cup for yourself?**
This can be done but sometimes it can be difficult to be impartial when it comes to reading for yourself.

11. **I turned my cup over, and there was barely anything in it? Does that mean I have no future?**

No. There can be a few factors as why this has occurred. Perhaps you didn't leave enough sediment on the bottom of the cup or you may have let the coffee go cold before turning it over. Perhaps you did not drink enough of the coffee, and the excess liquid resulted in all the sediment pouring out of the cup. It's best to drink another cup.

12. **The cup was quite dark and barely any shapes due to the thick dark sediment. What does that mean?**

This can be caused by drinking too much of the liquid portion of the coffee, thus leaving only the thick sediment. This can also mean that the cup drinker is enduring a difficult time in their life and are full of "heavy" thought/s.

13. **Is it ok to read my own cup after someone else has read my cup for me?**

No, it is best not to try to read your cup after someone else has provided you with a reading. It is said to bring you bad luck.

14. **Can I have sugar in my coffee or does this affect the reading?**

It is perfectly fine to have sugar in your coffee. This does not affect your reading.

15. **I tried to perform a reading but I couldn't see or feel a single thing. I was completely "blank"? What does that mean?**

If you try to read a cup and come up with a complete blank, that's ok. Just leave it for now as you may have worries on your mind or you may be too preoccupied with something else. Try to clear your mind and try again at a later date.

GULDJIN MILLER

10.   MEANING OF SYMBOLS

****

A

Acorn   Saving for something
                           important.

Adam/Eve   A new person will enter,
                           which will be a catalyst for
                           new paths in your life.

Air   Represented by a clear patch
                           in the cup. This means that
                           everything is fine and you have

no worries/problems during this patch.

Alarm Bell　This is a warning sign. You need to think about what you are doing, as it will cause you problems later.

Album　A photo album represents that you are remembering the past. Depending on what is next to this symbol indicates whether it is a happy or sad event.

Alien　An unusual person will be entering into your life shortly.

Anchor　If it is swinging, it means you are thinking about moving. If it is stable, you will stay where you are.

Angel　A guardian angel is with you. You are protected.

Anger　To see someone angry represented just that. Depending on what or who is near them depends on what they are angry about.

Ants

A group of people working together as a team to complete a common goal.

Anvil

A shock coming out of nowhere.

Anxiety

To see a person anxious represents just that. Depending what is near them, this will indicate what they are anxious about.

Ape/s

If they are playful, it is someone who is enjoying themselves and having fun. If they are serious, it denotes that someone who is usually care free is upset about something.

Apple

See "FRUIT."

Apricot

See "FRUIT."

Apron

Getting ready to begin a new project.

Arrow

A new direction.

Automobile	This could represent many things. It could indicate either: A new car; A journey (if it is at the beginning of a road); A car which will breakdown (if the hood is up or tire blown). Also if the car is light in color except for a certain spot, that can represent where the mechanical problem is; If it is completely light in color, the color of the car will be a light color; If slightly darker, the color of the car will be of a darker nature; If there are clouds or dark lumps around the car, it will be a bad purchase; It is a good purchase if it is clear around the car.
Axe	Cutting away people and negative influences in your life. This is a good symbol to see, as it represents cleansing.

B

Baby and /or Pram	Represents a new baby or a new start.
Bag-pipes	Someone of Scottish decent will enter your life.
Baking	Conjuring up a plan or project.
Ball	Getting the ball rolling of a project/goal.
Balloon	A joyful event.
Banjo	Feeling happy about an outcome.
Banana	See "FRUIT."
Banner	An announcement.
Barefoot	Standing on new ground. Going somewhere you have not been before.

Barrel

If the barrel is closed or empty, a potential problem is under control. If the lid is off and things are coming out of it, be ready for a whole lot of trouble coming your way.

Basin

Problems will soon disappear. Your emotions will settle down, and you will feel a new sense of calm regarding a situation.

Basket

You will receive many gifts.

Bat

You will receive bad news.

Bath

You can control your emotions over a situation.

Beacon-light

You will be guided regarding a problem.

Beans

From little things, big things will grow. Very positive.

Bear

Someone you know or meet is quite assertive and grumpy. This usually applies to someone in a work situation. This person is best avoided, as they will not change.

Beaver   Busily working away at a project.

Bed   Seeing someone in bed represents an illness and/or visiting someone in hospital. If you see their body rising from the bed, this represents death for this person.

Bees   One bee means that someone will help you achieve a goal. A swarm of bees means that a group of people will assist you.

Beetle   Secretly working hard at something.

Beggar   Someone wants or needs your help with something.

Beheading   A person will not be able to gossip/talk about you. They will be stopped by a person or event.

Bell/s   One bell – a marriage.
Two bells – good news.

Belly   A pregnant belly represents a
pregnancy.

Belt   A loose belt means a
comfortable lifestyle.
A tight belt means struggling
with finances.

Bench   Timeout from a problem or
event.

Bereavement   A person crying or upset
represents a sad event
occurring.

Bicycle   This could either be a new
bike or a short journey.

Bird/s   One bird represents news or a
letter. Many birds mean that
you will receive a lot of news.
If the birds are light in color, it
is good news. If dark, it is bad
news. For official news, SEE
"EAGLE."

Bird's Nest   If there are eggs in the nest, there will be a delay in news reaching you. If there are baby birds waiting for a feed, more information is required before it reaches you. This also applies if a bird is sitting in the nest.

Birth   Birth of a new baby or event.

Birthday Cake   A birthday party or celebration.

Blacksmith   A person will assist you with getting a promotion or excelling in something.

Blanket   Something is hidden from you.

Blindfold   You or someone else is unable to see what is happening.

Blossoms   Happiness. Your heart will bloom. See "FLOWER."

Boa-constrictor   An enemy will stop you from achieving a goal.

Boat	A boat represents many things: A new boat; experiencing an emotional period in your life; a journey by boat/ship; If the boat is travelling on rough water, you will feel quite emotional; If the water is calm, emotions are calm and relaxed. You can apply one of these choices, depending on what other symbol is next to the boat.
Bones	Something from your past will resurface. Something you thought would not resurface again. This does not necessarily represent a bad situation.
Books	Study.
Boots	Making your mark.
Bottle/s	Empty bottle/s represents a hollow victory. Full bottles signify a positive victory.

Bouquet — You will receive a bunch of flowers or extreme happiness.

Bow on Gift Box — A gift will be given to you.

Bow and Arrow — A person will provide you with direction.

Box — Either a package will be received or an unexpected surprise.

Bracelet — You will receive a bracelet or will complete something.

Brain — You know the answer to a problem, but do not want to accept this.

Branch — An idea which will eventually affect your life in a positive way.

Bread — A peace treaty between two people/parties who are arguing/fighting.

Bride — There will be a wedding.

Bridge	A short cut.
Broom	Removing negative influences from your life.
Brush	This represents smoothing out any problems that have been confusing you.
Buffalo	A large solid person in your life which will assist and guide you.
Bugle	A big announcement.
Buildings	A house represents security. A tent is temporary security. Skyscraper buildings representing visiting a city.
Bull	Jumping into something without thinking about the consequences.
Burglars	You will either be burgled – so be careful; someone or a few people are sneaking around you. They are up to no good. I would normally associate the

latter to work colleagues.

Burial   The end of an event.

Bus   A bus trip will be taken.

Butterfly   From hard work, something
                    very good will be coming.

Buttons   Finding the solution to a
                    problem.

C

Cab   A very short journey will be
                    taken.

Cabbage   Many different emotions will
                    be felt for a situation or
                    person.

Cabin   Temporary security regarding
                    a situation/person but this is
                    fine, as a more permanent
                    situation will come of it.

Cage   A bird cage represents

someone stopping news from reaching you.

Cake   A birthday cake represents a celebration.

Calendar   A significant event will happen. If there are numbers on the calendar, this will let you know when the event may occur e.g., 7 might be the seventh month (July) or the 7th day.

Camera   Making a lasting impression on someone.

Camel   A long journey will be taken.

Camp   Temporary security.

Canal   Strong emotions regarding a certain situation.

Candle   Being given the light regarding a situation.

Canon   A large shock.

Canoe   Emotions which can be easily
                          swayed regarding outside
                          influences.

Candy   A minor event will make you
                          happy.

Cap   Someone or yourself is hiding
                          something from someone.

Car/s   This could represent many
                          things. It could indicate
                          either:

                          A new car;
                          A journey (if it is at the
                          beginning of a road);
                          A car which will breakdown (if
                          the hood is up or tire blown).
                          Also if the car is light in color
                          except for a certain spot, that
                          can represent where the
                          mechanical problem is;
                          If it is completely light in
                          color, the color of the car will
                          be a light color;
                          If slightly darker, the color of
                          the car will be of a darker
                          nature;

If there are clouds or dark
lumps around the car, it will
be a bad purchase;
It is a good purchase if it is
clear around the car.

Cards
Taking a gamble with
something. Depending on
what symbols are nearby,
depends on whether it will
have a positive or negative
outcome.

Cart
Travel will take longer than
expected.

Carrot
A positive goal will be dangled
in front of you.   The
opportunity is there for you to
obtain it.

Cash
Receiving money.

Castle
Will feel very secure and
powerful regarding a situation.

Cat
A false friend.

Caterpillar
Working hard to achieve a
goal. The outcome will be

successful.

Cattle	A sacrifice will be made.
Cauldron	A dark cauldron represents creating problems for someone or a situation. A light cauldron represents finding a solution to a problem.
Cave	Something or someone is hidden from you at the moment. It will come out into the open soon.
Chain/s	Feeling tied down to something or someone.
Chair	A new position will arise.
Champagne Glass	A celebration.
Chandelier	Seeing the light into something which will bring you great joy.
Chapel	A marriage will take place.

Cheese

Someone who not been truthful and has been causing problems will be found out.

Cherries

Fruits of your labor.

Cherubs

You have a guardian angel which is protecting you.

Chicken

Something productive.

Chimney

You will feel very secure about a situation. This is a positive sign.

Choir

News will make you very happy.

Christmas Tree

Your life will be joyous and full of happiness.

Circle

Completing something.

Clam

A situation is closed to you. You will not be able to find out what you need to so you can succeed.

Claw

Enemy.

Climbing	Climbing a mountain or a ladder - if you reach the top you will succeed in an endeavor. If you fall or falter, reaching a goal will not occur.
Clock	Time is significant to an event.
Clouds	Dark clouds signify a negative period. Light clouds represent a negative period/situation that will soon be over. Worries will soon disappear.
Clover	Affection.
Coffin	A death will occur or the end to a situation.
Coin/s	Money is coming your way.
Comet	Significant news will reach you very quickly.
Cot	A birth of a child.
Cows	You will have a job which pays you well.

Crab

If the crab has large nippers, beware as someone is trying to take something away from you. Little nippers represents that they will not succeed.

Creek

Emotions will lead you onto a new path.

Crocodile

A sly person is saying negative things about you.

Cross

A contract will be signed.

Cross-bones

Be very careful about someone from your past.

Cross Roads

You will need to decide between two new paths.

Crow

You will receive bad news.

Crowd

You will go out to an event where there will be many people.

Crown

An achievement will be acknowledged, and many people will congratulate you.

Crucifix	You will have protection.

D

Daisy	You will be very happy in love.
Deer	Someone will be timid about a situation.
Desk	If there is one person sitting at the desk, they will be working very hard. If there are two people, a deal will be made.
Devil	A person will be up to no good.
Diamond/s	Either jewelry will be received or something precious to someone will be found out.
Dice	A chance will be taken. Light dice represent a positive outcome. Dark dice represents a negative outcome.

Dinosaur	Someone from your past will reappear.
Diploma	Someone will graduate.
Diving	Someone will either go diving or looking into emotions.
Doctor	A visit to the doctor or some news regarding someone's health will be heard soon.
Dog/s	A dog represents a friend. A puppy represents a new friend.
Dollar Sign	Money will be received.
Dolphin	Positive emotions will be felt regarding a situation. A very positive outcome will occur.
Donkey	Someone will be stubborn regarding a situation/person.
Door	A new situation/event will be opened. A dark door represents a negative situation. A light door represents a positive situation.

Doorbell   A new situation will present itself to you. It will be up to you whether you take it.

Doves   News of a wedding will be heard.

Dragon   Someone will be bad tempered regarding a situation.

Driving   You will start a new journey where you will be in control.

Drowning   To see someone drowning means that the person or someone else will feel overwhelmed in a situation. Look at the other symbols near this to see the reasons.

Duck   Someone will be moving their house.

Dwarf   To see a pleasant looking dwarf means that you will not be undermined in a situation. You will stand your own ground. To see an evil looking dwarf means that someone will make you feel small in a situation.

Dying

To see someone dying can either represent someone passing away or that a situation will end. Please look at the symbols around this to give you more guidance.

Dynamite

A situation will explode and cause many problems for those involved.

E

Eagle

Official news regarding business or government will be received.

Ear

A light ear represents hearing positive news. A dark ear represents hearing negative news.

Earrings

This is a good omen as it means there is interesting

work before you. If they are broken, this indicates that negative gossip will be directed against you.

Earwig

To see one or have on in your ear means that you will have unpleasant news affecting your business or family relations.

Eating

To see yourself eating alone and your plate is full, will mean that you will reap what you sow. A positive sign that something you have done will be successful and fruitful. To be eating with someone either means that you will be sharing the victory or it could mean a date (depends if there is a love heart close by).

Eclipse

Something is hidden from you, usually means someone is having an affair.

Eel

Someone will try to get involved with you regarding a financial situation. This person is only concerned about themselves. A business agreement should not be entered into with this person.

Egg/s

The beginning of a new project/s.

Elephant

A miracle that is so large that the person thought that it would be almost impossible for it to come true – but it will.

Elevator

If it is going up, moving up in career and/or life. Going down means the opposite.

Embrace

To see a couple embracing will mean a couple coming together romantically. I can also mean a farewell if there is a plane or boat next to it.

Emerald

You will inherit property, but there will be some trouble from others. If the opposite sex offers you an emerald, this means that they have more to offer than the person you are currently in a relationship with (or the person you are currently interested in).

Emperor   A successful and powerful man will help you in some way.

Empress   A successful and powerful woman will help you in some way.

Envelope   To see an envelope means you will receive some news. If the letter is light in color, it will be good news. If it is dark, the news will be negative.

Eye   Someone is watching you. An eye also means that someone is envious of you. A snake eye means that someone is very jealous of you.

Eyebrows   You will encounter sinister obstacles in your immediate future.

Eyeglass   Looking closely into a situation.

F

Face

If this person is recognized by the reader, depending on what is the near them, depends on why they are in your cup. If a face is half hidden by a dark patch, this means someone is not showing themselves completely. They are hiding something.

Fairy

Needed help will be received regarding a situation.

Fall

To see someone falling denotes that the person will "fall into a situation." Something not planned.

Fan

A cooling off period regarding a situation will occur.

Farewell

To see someone waving goodbye means that someone will leave from your life. To see a group of people means that you will be leaving.

Feather
You will hear part of some news or a secret and will have to search and dig for the rest of the news.

Feet
Landing on both feet regarding a situation. A positive outcome.

Fence
Boundaries will be laid out regarding a situation.

Ferry
A ferry ride will be taken or assistance in an emotion situation.

Festival
You will go to a social event with many people. You will have a good time.

Fiddle
Someone will stir trouble and will enjoy the outcome.

Fight
To see two people fighting denotes a disagreement.

Figs
This means good health. For a young woman's cup, this

denotes that she will marry a wealthy and prominent man.

Fingers

To see beautiful fingers means that your love will be requited. If the fingers are cut off, you will lose wealth due to enemies. To see long fingernails means that you will receive much love.

Fire

An ongoing argument with someone will re-erupt.

Fireman

Someone will be very lucky for you.

Fish

Luck and money will be received. The bigger the fish, the larger the amount.

Fisherman

Someone will help you attain money and wealth.

Fishhook/s

Luck will be "caught," which will bring money.

Fish Net

Assistance with getting some money.

Fish-pond Full of fish represents a lot of luck and money coming your way. An empty pond represents that the potential for money/luck is there for the person, they just need to trust their instincts.

Flag A victory.

Flame The beginning of an argument. Try and solve this argument quickly, otherwise a good relationship will be ruined.

Flower A situation/event will make you very happy. Your heart will bloom.

Flute A problem will be solved and a happy outcome will occur.

Flying To see someone flying means that they will feel free from a situation they have felt trapped in. It's a positive sign.

Fog There is a situation which is hidden. If it is thick, then it will be hidden for a while. If it seems to be "moving," things will come out into the open.

Forest

This denotes that the person feels lost and they are unhappy in their personal or work life and they are not sure how to fix it. Look for symbols close by to provide some guidance in regards to solving this problem.

Fork

Visitors will arrive.

Fountain

If it is clear around the fountain, this means vast possessions and an extremely enjoyable life. A broken fountain means insincerity of associates and unhappy love affairs.

Fox

Someone around you is sly and should not be trusted.

Frog

A gossip. To catch a frog is to catch someone out for gossiping about you. To see it eating a fly means that it keeps adding to the current gossip circulating.

Fruit

Represents the fruits of your labor. The positive result for the hard work you have done.

Funeral

A death or an end to a situation.

G

Gas Lamp

This means progress and pleasant surroundings. You will be happy in a certain situation.

Gate

Opportunities for success.

Garland

Success.

Geese

A jealous person will gossip about you and you will find out.

Gems

You will be successful in life.

Ghost

Something or someone from

your past will reappear. It will be a shock.

Giant   Someone with higher authority will assist you.

Gift   You will receive a gift.

Gloves   Someone is not showing you what they are up to. This is not necessarily a negative symbol. They may be doing something to help you. Light gloves are positive. Dark gloves are negative.

Goat   A sacrifice will need to be made.

Goblet   A celebration due to a successful outcome to a situation.

Gold   To see gold means that you will be very successful. A very good omen.

Goldfish   A small amount of money is coming your way.

Grapes

An achievement will give you quite a few things and/or opportunities. Very positive sign.

Grass

Long grass represents that certain things are being hidden from you. Short grass represents that you are aware of a certain situation, and therefore you can control the outcome.

Grasshopper

Someone will assist you regarding a situation by obtaining information or items that you need.

Grave

A death or an end to a situation.

Guitar

Something or someone needs to be handled with care.

Gun

An unexpected surprise will be received. It will come as a shock.

Gypsy

Someone footloose and carefree. Do not depend on

them, as they are not reliable.

H

Hammer   You will have to work hard to achieve something.

Hand/s   Someone will assist you with a project or a situation.
*See Fingers.

Handcuffs   Your hands will be tied regarding a situation.

Handwriting   A contract will be signed; this can either be a job contract (if there is a horse or chair nearby), a purchase of a large item like a house or car (there should be a symbol of either one close by), or a legal document (if the contract symbol is quite long in length).

Hair   To see beautiful long hair, someone is careless in their professional life and due to this, they will suffer from failure. To see thinning hair, someone is worrying excessively. To cut hair, there will be a serious disappointment. To see someone brushing hair, this means that someone is taking care of something of importance and this will work well for them.

Hare   A timid person.

Harp   Everything will be joyous and peaceful.

Hat   Someone is disguising their true intentions.

Hawk   Official news will be received. This will be some form of business or government news.

Head   To see the back of someone's head means that they are thinking of you but are still not wanting to come (back) into your life.

Hearse A death will be heard.

Heart Someone is in love with you. A heart with a crack in it represents heartbreak.

Hen Nurturing a project and working hard to bring it to fruition.

Hills Obstacles will be faced regarding a goal.

Hive To see a bee hive denotes that many people will help you achieve your dreams.

Hog/s Taxation department.

Hood Some one's true intensions are hidden.

Hook If the hook is empty, an opportunity will be missed. If the hook has something on it, this represents good luck.

Horse A promotion. A race horse denotes that you will move up the corporate ladder quite quickly.

Horseshoe If the ends of the horse shoe are pointing up, you will receive a pay rise. If the ends are pointing down, you will be unlucky in your job and there will be a loss.

Hospital To see someone in a hospital bed means that someone will have surgery and/or someone will require medical assistance. If things are clear around them, they will be fine. If there is a dark cloud, there will be some problems.

Hotel You will have an enjoyable evening outing.

House Security; if there is a contract next to it; you will purchase a new home.

Hunting To see someone hunting denotes that they are determined to achieve something. If you can see them attaining something, they will be successful.

Hurricane   A major change in your life will occur. If it is clear afterwards, it will be a good change. If it is dark, it will mean a negative change.

Hut   You will be successful in something, but it won't make you happy. You thought that it would but once attained, you will be indifferent.

Hyena   Someone will be untrustworthy. If there are two, lovers will quarrel. To see one attacking, someone will attack your integrity.

I

Ice Cream   A taste of small success early on into a project.

Icicle/s   A situation which cannot be changed.

Infant   A birth or a new project.

Injury   To see someone injured
                      denotes that an unfortunate
                      incident will occur.

Inn   Temporary security regarding
                      a situation.

Intestine   If there is a dark spot in the
                      intestines, there is a tumor (or
                      blockage) in this area and
                      needs medical assistance.

Intoxicated   Someone will not be able to
                      see things clearly or the way
                      they truly are. They are
                      blinded to a situation.

Iron   Solving little problems
                      regarding a situation.

Island   This denotes comfort and easy
                      circumstances after much
                      striving and worrying to meet
                      obligations.

Ivy   A project will take shape and
                      then will suddenly take off
                      very quickly.

J

Jail   Someone will go to jail or not being able to stop an event/situation from happening.

Jar   Bottling up emotions which will eventually come out.

Jaws   Shark jaws represents that someone is out to get you. This does not mean physically. This is usually in the work place.

Jester   Someone will be joking around regarding a situation.

Jewelry   You will receive jewelry. To see it broken, you will have disappointment in attaining something highly desired.

Jewels   Great success and happiness is coming your way.

Jockey   Someone will assist you with a promotion.

Journey   If you see someone at the start of a road and the path is clear, a trip will be good. If you see obstacles, it will have issues.

Judge   A decision you have been waiting on will finally be made.

Jug   Emotions regarding a situation will flow. This is quite cleansing and healing. If the jug is full, it will be quite an emotional situation.

Jury   You will be judged regarding a situation.

K

Kangaroo   A situation will stop and start.

Kettle   You will receive assistance with something you thought was impossible. Someone will help you make it possible.

Key

You will purchase an item which requires a new key e.g. car, house, etc. The shape of the key will help you to decide what item it is.

Keyhole

An opportunity will arise, but you will have to work harder to make something happen.

Kidneys

Someone will have kidney problems.

King

A boss or someone in charge will help you in some way.

Kiss

To see two people kissing means that they are in loving relationship. If the person is single, they will soon be in a loving relationship.

Kite

Care free period.

Kitten

A new enemy. It will be someone who you have recently met and they will act like a friend, but secretly they do not like you.

Knife

You will be stabbed in the back by someone you thought you could trust.

Knitting

Someone will cause problems for you.

L

Ladder

Moving up in your job or a project.

Ladle

Someone will stir up trouble for you.

Lagoon

Deep emotions regarding a situation.

Lake

Overwhelming emotions will be sorted out.

Lamb

A sacrifice will be made.

Lamp   Guidance will be given.

Lantern   Past influences will guide you
                      regarding a situation.

Laughing   To see someone laughing or a
                      group of people laughing
                      means an enjoyable situation.
                      An enjoyable outing.

Leaking Tap   Something will happen slowly.

Leaves   Leaves on the ground is the
                      end to a situation, project.
                      Leaves on a tree represent a
                      project, business, or situation
                      succeeding and being fruitful.

Lemon/s   Someone is sour about a
                      situation.

Letter   If the letter is light in color,
                      you will receive good news in
                      the mail. If dark, the news will
                      not be good.
                      If there is a dollar sign or fish
                      next to it, you will receive
                      news that you have come into
                      some money.
                      If there is a coffin or cross,

you will receive news of a
death.

Lettuce

No matter how hard you try
regarding a situation, you will
not be able to get to the root
of the problem.

Life-Boat

You will receive support
regarding your emotions about
a person/situation.

Lighthouse

Guidance will be given
regarding an emotional
situation.

Lightning

You will receive an
unexpected shock. Depending
on what symbols are next to
this, will determine whether it
is good or not and what it is
regarding.

Lily

The end of something will
bring happiness.

Lines

If line is straight, trouble free
progress. If it's wavy, then it
points out difficult progress.

Lion	A fiery character will make an impact into your life.
Lips	Light colored lips represents that someone is saying good things about you.
Liver	Someone will have problems with their liver.
Lizard	A person is plotting against you, even though you think they are on your side. Beware.
Lobster	A wealthy person will assist you with a project/problem.
Lock	If there is no key nearby, you will have problems finding the solution to a problem.
Locket	Hidden affection for someone.
Looking-glass	Looking closely at a situation.
Love heart	To see a light colored love heart; someone is in love with you. To see a dark spot on the heart, someone is having concerns about a relationship.

If the heart has a crack in it, there is a broken relationship or heartbreak. If the heart looks like an actual body part (heart), someone has issues with their heart, and they need to get some medical attention.

Luggage

Indicates travel. If there is water next to the luggage, it represents travel overseas.

Lump

A lump in your cup represents obtaining something large in value. Depending on the size of the lump, it could represent a purchase of a large item for the home or buying a house or land.

M

Magnet

Something or someone will be drawn to you. You will receive what you want without trying too hard.

Magpie — News of a jealous person.

Man — This could represent many things, depending on what is next to this symbol or what the man is doing. It is best to use your intuition. Sometimes the reader will recognize the man or will be able to see facile features quite clearly. Look at what this man is wearing. If wearing sunglasses, this means that a man is disguising his true intentions. If there is a capital letter next to this man, his name begins with this letter. If the letter is lower case, this letter appears in his name.

Mansion — You will feel extremely secure and happy with life. A very good symbol. It also represents wealth.

Map — You will receive guidance.

Mare — You will get a promotion.

Marriage   You will either go to a
wedding or you feel very
secure in your relationship.

Mask   Someone is hiding their true
feelings or intentions towards
the person who is having their
cup read.

Mat   Someone is taking advantage
of you. Be careful not to let
people walk all over you.

Match   To see a lit match represents
unexpected news, and fortune
is on its way.

Medal   An achievement.

Mermaid   A female will be very lucky for
you.

Mice   Someone is working hard to
help you. This usually
represents work, but it could
also represent your personal
life.

Mirror	Taking a good look at yourself and make changes. Sometimes we do not realize that we are behaving in a certain way.
Mistletoe	You will receive a kiss from someone who you are attracted to.
Money	A money bag, dollar notes, or dollars sign represents just that. You will come into some money. The size of the symbol will determine the amount of money you will receive. Obviously, a large money bag or dollar size represents quite a lot of money, just as a small symbol represents a small amount of money being received.
Monkey	Experiencing a persistent problem.
Moon (full)	A complete change will occur in your life.

Moon (half)   A new phase in your life.

Moth   Quarrels in a relationship will occur.

Mouse-trap   You will catch someone out who has been pretending to help you when they have been doing the complete opposite.

Musical Instrument   Happiness.

Musical Note   Also represents Happiness.
Mushroom   A project/relationship will grow and expand. Very positive symbol.

Mountain   A situation seems quite daunting. It will require quite a bit of effort to get over or to reach.

Mouse   Someone is working hard to help you. This usually represents work, but it could also represent your personal life.

Mouse trap

A person who is trying to help you will have their attempts stopped or delayed.

Moustache

A male friend is secretly attracted to you. You think that you are just good friends.

N

Necklace

This could either mean that a necklace will be received or a relationship will move to the next level. Look for other symbols nearby to give you a clearer answer.

Needle

You will make up with someone that you have had a disagreement with.

Nest

This represents ideas that have not come to fruition. They are good ideas, and can be quite successful.

Newspaper You will hear news second hand.

Nose Someone will put their nose into your business.

Nuns Someone is saying prayers for you. This is a good omen.

Nuptial Seeing people getting married is a great sign that the person will be getting engaged soon. If already married, a long awaited promise made by their partner will finally be given.

Nurse To see a nurse represents that someone will be ill, but that they will recover quite quickly. It can also mean a visit to the doctor.

Nuts To see a group of nuts represents a successful enterprise and much favor in love. To see someone eating nuts means that they will experience amazing success and riches.

O

Oar

Having one oar represents going around in circles regarding your emotions. This also represents confusion. Two oars represent sorting through your emotions and coming out feeling satisfied.

Ocean

Water represents emotions. Calm water represents feeling in control, happy, and serene. Rough water represents confusion, unhappiness, and sadness. To see fish swimming in the ocean represents many opportunities that will present themselves.

Old Man/ Woman

Guidance will be received from an unlikely source.

Olives

To see them denotes good friends and happy times. To eat them signifies contentment and faithful friends.

Opera   To see a person singing at an opera denotes that you will be entertained by congenial friends, and find that your immediate affairs will be favorable.

Oranges   See "FRUIT."

Orchard   To see an orchard full of fruit means that the person will be extremely successful and many opportunities will present themselves. Very good symbol.

Ostrich   News will be received by someone who does not want to face a situation. This news will be ignored.

Otter   To see them swimming means happiness and good fortune. If a woman's reading, it represents a very loving partner.

Overcoat   Someone will hide a project or idea they are working on. All will be revealed later on.

Ox

To see a well fed ox means that the person will rise to a position beyond their expectation. If the ox is thin and frail, this means that the person will not do very well in their career (even though they try quite hard). If the ox is dead, this is a sign of bereavement.

Owl

Someone wise and knowledgeable will assist you with a problem/situation.

Oysters

The source of a problem will be discovered.

P

Painting

Painting with a paint brush represents putting final touches to a project.

Palace   You will feel extremely secure and happy with life. A very good sign.

Palm Tree   A relaxing holiday will be taken.

Panther   Someone will pretend to be your friend but beware, as this person is able to cause quite a few problems if you let them. They are very sly.

Parcel   A parcel will be received.

Parrot   If the parrot is light in color, gossip of a light hearted nature will be heard. A dark colored parrot represents bad gossip.

Parsnip   To see them represents successful business. If eating them, it means that love will take an unfavorable and gloomy aspect.

Party   You will go to a party. If there are no negative symbols nearby, the party will be enjoyable.

Path

A clear white path represents a new project or idea that will be completed and will be successful. If the path is dark or blocked off at the end, this represents that the project/idea will not be completed as there will be problems. Sometimes, the path can branch into two paths. This means a choice will need to be made.

Peace Pipe

The end of an argument.

Peaches

See "FRUIT."

Peacock

This is a very lucky symbol. It means that something wonderful is coming into your life which will make you very happy.

Pearls

A pearl necklace represents either a necklace being received or a couple getting very serious. It could mean that either the couple purchase a house together, move in together, or make a significant commitment to one another. This does not mean engagement.

Pear   SEE "Fruit."

Peas   Signifies robust health and accumulation of wealth.

Pebbles   There will be a few hiccups with an idea, but they will be solved.

Pelican   You will receive a lot of information regarding a situation or event.

Pen   A contract will be signed. This will be binding.

Pencil   A draft contract will be signed, but will not be binding due to a loophole. It can be broken.

Penny   Unsatisfactory pursuits. Business will suffer and lover/s and friends will complain of the lack of affection from you.

Pepper

To see it burning your tongue, foretells that the person will suffer from acquaintances through your love of gossip.

People

A group of people represents an event where there are many people e.g., a concert, theatre, etc. Such an event will be attended.

Pheasant

Something unusual will become productive. An unconventional idea will work even though some doubt may be associated with it.

Piano

Either a piano will be received/purchased or someone will bring a lot of happiness into the person's life.

Pickles

You will follow worthless pursuits. It indicates an unambitious person.

Pies   Trying hard to impress someone/something. This will be successful.

Pig   This represents the Taxation Department (IRS).

Pigeon   Gossip or false information will be written about you in the paper.

Pill   Finding a solution to a problem. Be careful, as it is only a "quick fix."

Pillow   Trust your dreams for a solution to a problem.

Pineapple   See "FRUIT."

Pine Tree   The growth of a project. Positive symbol.

Pirate   Be careful of your belongings, as this represents a thief.

Pistol   A shock will be received.

Pitchfork   A difficult decision will need to be made. There are a few options, which is causing you problems and making the decision difficult to make.

Plane
A plane facing away from the handle (clockwise) represents someone leaving.

Facing the handle (anti-clockwise) represents someone arriving by plane.

If the plane is large, it has travelled a large distance. If you see water under the plane, it means that it has flown from overseas. A small plane represents a small journey – usually intrastate travel.

Plate
You will be given something that most people need to struggle for. It could be a job, promotion, or opportunity. This is a very good symbol.

Plow
Working hard to achieve a goal.

Plum
See "FRUIT."

Polar Bear

A person cannot be trusted. This person has some authority – usually a boss or someone with wealth. They may appear to be OK, but they are very cold and will use you to their advantage (if you let them). Be warned.

Police

Some involvement with the police or justice will be served regarding a situation. Depends on what symbol is next to this.

Pony

A minor promotion or job change will occur.

Postage

A letter will be received. Dark in color is negative news. Light in color is positive news.

Pot

If the pot is boiling, someone is planning something regarding you. If you can see someone next to the pot – it means that this person is plotting against you.

Witches near a boiling pot represents that good things are coming your way regarding a matter that you would want to happen.

Prayer

Someone is looking out for you. Your guardian angel is protecting you. This is a very good omen.

Pregnant Woman

Someone you know is pregnant.

Present

A gift will be received.

Priest

If the priest is dark in color, you will hear of a death. Light in color means that you are protected and someone is praying for you.

Puddle

Someone's feelings for you are not as deep as you had hoped, or thought.

Puppy

You will make a new friend.

Purse

If the purse looks empty, you will have some financial

difficulties. If it looks full, you will receive either a pay increase or some other financial gain which will be ongoing.

Q

Quail

A slight person is gossiping about you.

Quarrel/s

This denotes unhappiness and disagreements.

Queen

A nice looking queen represents gaining control of a situation. You are in charge. An evil looking queen represents that another women is in control of a situation involving you. This usually represents a relationship.

Quicksand

Beware. Be careful of a situation. This represents

failure. You will feel as though you do not have control over a situation.

R

Rabbit

This represents being timid regarding a situation.

Raccoon

This means you are being deceived by someone who is pretending to be your friend, and you can't tell because of their friendly nature.

Race

Competing with other people for something. It may be a job, a person, etc. Whatever you want. Other people also want this.

Radish

Your anticipations will be happily realized.

Raffle Ticket

You will win something involving a raffle ticket.

Sometimes a symbol will appear near this to show what you will win. A house, car, boat, dollar sign, etc.

Raft

Feeling unsure of your feelings regarding someone or a situation.

Railroad

You will need to decide on which direction to take regarding a matter.

Rain

Depending on what symbol is nearby, this could represent: Rain on a special day (e.g., Wedding day) or; Tears regarding a situation or; Feeling many different emotions regarding a situation or person.

Rainbow

A successful outcome to a difficult situation.

Rake

Many options will open up for you, and you may find it difficult to choose a path.

Ram   A large sacrifice will need to be made.

Rapids   If you see someone being carried over rapids that denote that the person will suffer an appalling loss due to courting with seductive pleasures.

Rat   Be careful of someone who only thinks of themselves.

Rattle   A baby's rattle represents the birth of a child or an announcement of a pregnancy.

Razor   You will be able to remove any obstacles without much difficulty regarding a situation.

Refrigerator   Your selfishness will offend and injure someone who is trying to gain an honest livelihood.

Register   If you own a business, it will be successful if the register is light in color. If dark in color, you will face financial difficulties. If you do not own a business, you will purchase one.

Reindeer A surprise visit from someone at Christmas time.

Reptile See "SNAKE" or "LIZARD."

Ribbon A lovely gift will be received.

Ring Two wedding rings linked together represent a wedding. An engagement ring (with a diamond on top) represents an engagement. A single ring represents a completion of a project or event.

River A flowing river represents emotions about an event or person. Depending on what symbol is next to this. A person near this would represent the person having the reading. They have feelings for this person.

Riding Horse To ride a horse represents someone showing off an achievement or promotion.

Ringworm   You will have a slight illness,
                      but will be fine.

Rising Sun   After a difficult time, the sun
                      will finally shine. A positive
                      change.

River   A clear flowing river
                      represents success and easy
                      progress. To see an
                      overflowing river represents
                      emotions overflowing. To see
                      blockages in the river
                      represents emotional
                      challenges.

Road/s   This represents paths that will
                      be taken and completed, if
                      clear, at the end. If they do
                      not stretch the length of the
                      cup (vertically) and stop
                      halfway, then the project/path
                      will not be completed.

Rocking Chair   You will be undecided
                      regarding a position which will
                      be offered to you.

Rocking Horse   A promotion will not be everything you expect. May be best not to accept the promotion as you will be disappointed.

Rocks   A pile of rocks denotes difficult times and unhappiness.

Roof   A roof of a house means that there is potential for security, but further work needs to be done to establish this.

Rooster   Represents an argument.

Roots   This means a strong foundation is laid. Either with work, friendship, or a relationship. It depends of what symbol is next to this.

Ropes   If the ropes are twisted or tied up, then you will feel like that you don't have control over a situation or a person's feelings. If they are hanging loose, this represents that you have the ability to control someone or something.

Rose/s

You will be very happy. See "FLOWER."

Rowboat

Represents that you or someone else is slowly sorting out their feelings regarding a person/situation. This person needs time, so do not rush things as this will cause them to go the other direction.

Running

If this symbol is light in color, someone will succeed in obtaining a goal ahead of other people. If dark in color, trying to outrun your problems will not work, facing them will sort them out a lot quicker.

S

Saddle

You will work temporarily in a higher position at work. You may replace your manager/boss while they are away, but it will only be until they return to work.

Safe

If the safe is locked, there are secrets that are being kept from you. If you have numbers near this or the safe door is open, you will be told this top secret information.

Sailing

If the water is smooth, you will be happy in your relationship with a partner. If the water is rough, there will be problems to overcome.

Sailor

You will either meet a sailor or someone who travels a lot will cross your path.

Salad

Eating salad denotes someone is being precautious about a situation. To make a salad means that your partner will be changeable and quarrelsome.

Sand

This represents a famine or losses.

Sapphire   A fortune will be gained.
Many riches. A very fortunate
symbol.

Satan   Someone will try to cause
problems for you. If near a
couple, this presents an affair.
Also See "DEVIL."

Saw   Someone is out to take
something from you which
you have worked hard for. It
may be your job, partner, or
friendship. Be aware and keep
your eyes open.

Scale   Weighing up your options
regarding a matter. If the
scales are balanced, the
outcome will be positive. If
unbalanced, some problems
will arise.

Scissors   Letting go of things/people
from your past that you no
longer require in your life.

School   Further study will be taken.

Scorpion   Be careful of an enemy.
Watch your back. They will
not be able to "get" you if you
keep your eyes open.

Sculptor   Take your time with a project
and you will be successful, as
you have the right skills to
achieve. Do not be too
anxious for the outcome,
otherwise this will cause you
to rush and you will not be
successful.

Sea   Deep emotions regarding a
person or situation. If there
are waves, the emotions are
controlling you. If the sea is
calm, your emotions are under
control.

Seal   A playful person in your life or
about to enter. They will be a
good acquaintance who makes
you happy. This person will
not be in your life for very
long.

Seat   A new position will be offered
to you. Depending on how

large the chair is, depends on
how important the position is.
If light in color, take the job.
If dark, it is not a good job.

Seed

A new idea will be formed and
will be successful if the person
can follow through. It will
bring money if nurtured.

Serpent

You have an enemy who has
made it clear they don't like
you.

Shaking Hands

A deal will be made.
Depending on what symbol is
nearby, depends on what the
deal was regarding.

Shark

You will receive money which
will leave your hands as
quickly as you get it. You may
need to pay bills or an
outstanding debt.

Sheep

A sacrifice will need to be
made.

Shells
You will have a holiday involving the ocean.

Ship
A large ship represents an ocean voyage. A small ship represents smooth sailing regarding a situation which has been causing you to worry.

Ship Wreck
Unrequited love.

Shoes
A high heel shoe represents an outing;
Walking shoes represents visiting a place you have not been to before;
Boots represents standing firm in a decision.

Shotgun
You will be told something that will shock you. If the gun is light in color, it will be a good surprise. If it is dark in color, it will not be so good.

Shovel
A situation or details of an event from your past will resurface. It will be something that you wish was forgotten.

Signature

An official document will be signed. It may be for a loan, new car etc.

Skates

You will find yourself in a position which you will be able to handle very comfortably. Do not worry. Everything is under control.

Skeleton

You will see someone from your past that you thought you would not see again. Very unexpected.

Skull

A problem from your past will resurface.

Smoke

Someone is trying to distract you from doing something. Depending on what symbol is near this, may indicate what they are stopping you from doing. It is not necessarily a bad symbol, but you will need to look carefully at what you are doing.

Snake

You have an enemy.

Snail

Something will take a long time to complete.

Snow

A person is unhappy with their situation. Although others view this person's life to be picture perfect, the person themselves is unsatisfied and unhappy.

Soap

Cleansing parts of your life. Removing people or items from your life which are either not good for you or you no longer need.

Soldier

Someone will either join one of the armed forces or you are protected.

Spade

You will try and hide something, but other people will find out. It could be either feelings or something you have done. It depends on what symbol is next to this.

Spectacles

You will get a clearer look at a situation. Seeing things much more clearly.

Spider Secretly working on a project.

Spider-web Trying discreetly to collect information about someone or a situation.

Spoon Achieving goals and money without much effort. These items will be given to you. Help from a third person. Beneficial.

Spy Someone is being secretive and also snooping around you.

Square You will not be able to cut corners regarding a situation.

Squirrel Represents someone who is tight with their money.

Stable Many job opportunities will open up for you. You will have a choice.

Stairs Ascending stairs represents "moving up" in the world. You will reach the next level in finances, love, etc. If the stairs are descending, the opposite applies.

Star   A wish will come true.

Storm   Dark clouds represent unhappiness. If the clouds appear to be parting, then the worst is over and things will improve.

Strawberries   See "FRUIT."

Sun   Power. Success. Rising sun means sudden success.

Sunglasses   Someone is hiding their true feelings or intension from you.

Spider   Denotes that someone will require surgery. Also denotes that someone will "cut" things out of their life.

Swan   News of love will soon be heard.

Sweeping   Reorganizing your life and priorities. This is a positive symbol.

Swimming   Swimming calmly represents being comfortable and happy with your emotions regarding a situation or person.   If you are drowning or having troubles swimming, you are feeling overwhelmed by your emotions.

Sword   Enemies will fall.

T

Table   A deal will be made and papers will be signed.

Tadpole   There will be gossip about your finances.

Tail   Someone is not showing you their true emotions.

Tambourine   A happy event.

Tank

Someone will try and force you to do something you do not really want to do. Stand firm in your decision.

Tea cup

A pleasurable experience. To see it broken denotes that a positive situation will be marred by a negative experience.

Tea Pot

A miracle will occur.

Tears

Tears will be shed. If they are light in color, they will be happy tears, while dark in color indicates great sadness.

Teeth

A visit to the dentist.

Telephone

You will receive a significant phone call.

Telephone Lines

This represents a telephone call from interstate. If the lines cross over water, a phone call from someone overseas will be received.

Telescope

Someone is watching you closely but from a distance. You may not be aware that they are watching you. This could be, for example, a boss who is quite high up in the organization.

Tent

Temporary security.

Tie

Happy news, such as engagement.

Tiger

Someone you know will have something stolen from them. You will be fine, but will need to be careful with your belongings. This is a warning.

Toad

Someone is spreading gossip about you which is exaggerated and untrue.

Tongue

A tongue, light in color, represents someone saying nice things about you. A dark colored tongue represents that someone is saying negative things about you.

Torch You will be given assistance with something you have wanted to find out.

Tower A goal is unreachable at the moment due to certain circumstances. Leave it for a while, and try again later on.

Toys An event which will prove to be most enjoyable.

Train Either a train journey will be taken or, if a money symbol is nearby, a business venture will do very well.

Trap You will catch someone out who is doing something dishonest against you or someone you know.

Treasure A very successful outcome to a situation. A lot of happiness will follow.

Tree/s Something you have worked hard for will be achieved. It will be stable and positive. Many years of hard work is normally involved with this symbol. Usually study or working your way up through a company. Your position will be comfortable.

Triangle

A love triangle exists between three people.

Trophy

You will be triumphant when competing with other people for a position or item.

Trumpet

An announcement will be made.

Trunk

If you have a key near this, something that has been unachievable previously is now within reach. If there is no key nearby, it is still out of reach.

Tub

Emotional healing.

Tunnel

If you can see a light at the end at the tunnel, it literally means this regarding a situation. If the tunnel is dark or blocked, you will not be able to find a solution to a problem and will concede defeat.

Turkey   Someone will try to boss you around, but will fail as they do not have any authority to do so.

Turtle   Help to a situation or problem may have been coming slowly but will finally arrive. A friend will be very helpful.

Twins   Someone you know is either having twins or if one of the twins is dark and the other light in color, this means that you will see two sides to someone (good and bad).

U

Umbrella   Protection from problems.

Underwear   One of your secrets will be revealed. Someone will find

out one of your secrets and
you will feel exposed.

Uniform   Depending on the uniform,
this will tell you what person
will be entering your life.

Unicorn   Someone will promise you a
promotion, but it will not be
given.

Urn   A miracle will occur not the
way you would expect. A very
good symbol.

V

Vase   If the vase is full of flowers,
you will be extremely happy.
If the vase is empty, a solution
to a problem will leave you
feeling empty and unsatisfied.

Vegetables   Productivity with a project or
situation.

Vehicle   See "MOTOR VEHICLE."

Veil   A pending marriage, which has
                            been kept a secret, will be
                            revealed.

Vine   Working towards a project will
                            take unexpected twists and
                            turns before you complete it.

Violets   You will be very happy
                            regarding a situation.

Volcano   A terrible argument will occur.
                            Someone's temper will
                            explode.

Vultures   You will receive news from a
                            debt collector.

Wagon   Completing a project or goal
                            will take a little longer than
                            anticipated. Unexpected
                            problems will arise, but they
                            can be overcome.

Waiter   You will receive assistance from someone you thought would not help you.

Walking Stick   Support will be given regarding a situation.

Wallet   A full wallet represents an increase in your pay packet. An empty wallet represents financial difficulties.

Wasp   Be careful of a gossip that can be harmful to you.

Watch   Time will be significant regarding a situation.

Water   See "OCEAN" and "WAVES."

Waterfall   Someone will "pour out" their heart to you and tell you how they feel.

Water Lily   Emotionally, you will be very happy.

Waves   Strong emotions regarding a person or situation.

Wedding   A wedding will occur.

Wedding Ring   You will hear of a wedding
                       taking place.

Whale   A large sum of money.

Whip   You will be forced to work
                       hard to achieve a goal.

Whirlpool   Losing control of your
                       emotions. Try to focus on
                       what is important to you.

Whirlwind   Something will happen very
                       quickly and will be quite
                       unexpected. You are not able
                       to slow things down. Go with
                       the flow.

Whispering   Secrets about you are being
                       told which are not true.

Whistle   Something will be brought to
                       your attention which you did
                       not notice before.

Wig   Someone will disguise their
                       true intentions, but you will be

able to see them for who or what they are. This is not necessarily a negative symbol.

Will   Someone will leave something for you in their will.

Wind   Change is coming.

Windmill   You will be driven by your emotions regarding starting a new project or goal.

Window   You will find out about a situation, but will not be able to change anything. It is beyond your control. You can only watch and wait.

Wishing Well   A wish will come true.

Witch   A "light" colored witch represents that someone is working towards helping you with a problem. A "dark" colored witch represents that someone is plotting against you. This person is female.

Wizard   This is the same as "Witch," but represents a male.

Wool   A sacrifice has been made and you will reap the rewards.

Worms   Digging deep to find some information and you will be find out what you want.

Y

Yacht   Sailing on calm water represents calm happy emotions. Sailing on rough water represents unsettled, confused emotions regarding a situation or person.

Yard Stick   You will feel quite anxious about a situation.

Yarn   Success in your business, and you will get help from within your home.

Yawning

An ongoing situation will become tiresome.

Yearning

To see someone "yearning" for something or something denotes that what they are wanting will be received soon.

Z

Zebra

A promotion will bring about a job that is completely different from what you are used to. You will not be sure about whether you want this job, as it is not something you had thought about doing. It will be good for you.

Zodiac

This symbol will represent a person with this particular star sign. Look at the symbols around this to give you an idea of what purpose this person will have.

ABOUT THE AUTHOR

Born in Nicosia, Cyprus, Guldjin Miller is a fourth generation psychic living in Australia. With over 30 years experience reading coffee cups, Guldjin developed her skills through her Turkish family. She has performed personal readings for clients for over 20 years and expanded her spiritual help into Tarot and Gypsy card readings.

Made in the USA
Las Vegas, NV
15 December 2021

37933382R00098